Original title:
Under the Veil of Lace

Copyright © 2025 Creative Arts Management OÜ
All rights reserved.

Author: Vivienne Beaumont
ISBN HARDBACK: 978-1-80586-012-9
ISBN PAPERBACK: 978-1-80586-484-4

The Filigree of Time's Caress

In a world of dainty threads,
Laughter dances on fine lace,
Tickling time on silly heads,
As we all join in the race.

Whispers floating through the air,
Like confetti, they drift and swirl,
Each giggle tastes like sweet despair,
For wrinkled socks and hair in whirl.

Glimmers caught in each bright smile,
Every moment an artful tease,
Fleeting joy makes life worthwhile,
We twirl around like playful bees.

With starlight caught in our own nets,
We riddle the night with our cheer,
As time forgets its vain regrets,
And laughter drowns out every fear.

Silken Echoes of Eternity

In the realm of silken dreams,
Chasing giggles down the hall,
Laughter bursts and brightly gleams,
Like a jester's vibrant call.

Draped in joy and silly cheer,
Every whisper spins a smile,
Weighing nothing but the sheer
Absurdity that lasts a while.

With shadows long and antics bright,
Our hearts will dance to playful tunes,
As time takes flight, we share the night,
And wiggle like the silly loons.

Oh, the fabric of our days,
Woven thick with laughter's thread,
In a tapestry of ways,
We stitch together fun instead.

Patterns in the Twilight

In twilight's glow, a cat prances,
Chasing shadows, taking chances.
A sneaky mouse just rolls its eyes,
Thinking of cheese, what a sweet surprise!

The stars above are winking bright,
As squirrels plot to steal the night.
With acorns stacked like tiny towers,
They giggle softly, mostly cowards.

Tangles of Light and Shadow

In knots of light, the dancers spin,
Twisting each limb, trying to win.
A slip, a trip, oh what a sight,
They can't recall who's left or right!

Shadows stretch with a silly grin,
Hiding secrets, plotting to win.
"Who stepped on me?" a voice complains,
While laughter bursts like summer rains!

The Dance of Fragile Aritistry

Delicate hands with flour and dough,
Creating pastries in a flow.
But flour flies in a playful brawl,
Cooks twirl like leaves in the fall!

With icing drips that paint the floor,
And lopsided cakes that the judges ignore,
Each dessert tells a story true,
Of mishaps shared by the whole crew!

Lattice of Hidden Yearnings

A garden grows, but weeds arrive,
The flowers giggle, trying to thrive.
"I can't see you!" a tulip shouts,
As clovers whisper about their doubts.

Beneath the leaves, secrets are sown,
A ladybug seeks a place called home.
Yet every petal, fluffs and flares,
Dreams of sunshine beneath the layers!

The Allure of Whispered Wishes

With dreams that dance in quiet nights,
A sprinkle of humor, oh what delights!
We giggle beneath the moon's gentle glow,
As wishes float by, like soft flakes of snow.

A wink to the stars, a jest unfolds,
Tales of mischief, in laughter we're told.
A promise of joy, wrapped oh so tight,
In the fabric of giggles, we take our flight.

Chasing Silhouettes of Serenity

In a world of calm, where shadows play,
We stumble on giggles, in the light of day.
Chasing our laughs as they prance and twirl,
In this dance of silliness, we spin and whirl.

With whispers of joy, and a wink of an eye,
We're crafting our moments, as time floats by.
A tickle of laughter, a chase we embrace,
In these fleeting antics, we find our place.

Beneath a Canvas of Intricacy

Life's tangled threads weave stories so bright,
With quirks and mishaps that bring us delight.
Like artists with brushes, we paint with our jest,
In the gallery of life, humor's the best.

We trip on our hopes, then burst into glee,
Turning falls into frolic, just wait and see!
Each moment's a portrait, a laugh we can trace,
In the chaos, we find our unique grace.

Cloaked in Romantic Enigma

Wrapped in a riddle, with chuckles to share,
A tapestry woven with wit and with flair.
Love plays the jester, with a wink and a grin,
In this comedic court, we're destined to win.

With secret exchanges and playful deceit,
Each glance is a giggle, our hearts skip a beat.
Like shadows entwining, with laughter we tease,
In this playful drama, we aim to please.

A Scherzo in Silk

A dance of fabric twirls in delight,
Laughing at shadows that flirt with the light.
Silken whispers tickle the air,
As patterns engage in a playful affair.

A slip of the hand, oh what a surprise!
Caught in a moment, we giggle and rise.
The lace takes a bow, a comical sight,
As we weave our mischief in sheer delight.

The Mystery of Ornate Embrace

Beneath the folds, secrets do play,
An ornate hug hides jokes on display.
What's lost in the seam? Just a silly grin,
As twists and turns invite us to spin.

With each little flutter, we stop and we stare,
An unraveling tale of extravagant flair.
It's all just a riddle, or so it seems,
A puzzle of laughter and fancy dreams.

Threads of Timeless Beauty

Threads of humor lace through the fine,
Woven in patterns designed to confine.
But oh, what a riot, we find in the fold,
As laughter erupts in colors bold!

A stitch in time saves a joke on the run,
When beauty is quirky, it's all rather fun.
A tapestry chuckles, with mischief it beams,
Creating a masterpiece tangled in dreams.

Enfolded in Tenderness

In softness we giggle, entrapped in the fray,
Tenderness teasing, in a whimsical way.
The fabric quivers, it starts to beguile,
As we tumble through laughter, forget the style.

Embraced by the threads, we stumble and fall,
Wrapped in the warmth, we're having a ball.
The lace catches grins that bloom from the heart,
In a playful ensemble, we each play our part.

Raindrops on Petals of Tulle

Raindrops dance on fabric light,
Puddles laugh in soft delight.
Frills and giggles, quite a sight,
Petals blush in morning bright.

A bee stumbled on lace so fine,
Buzzing, bumping, saying, 'Mine!'
The flowers whisper, 'What a line!'
While moments twirl like grapevine.

A Tangle of Threads and Dreams

A ball of yarn rolls down the hall,
Chasing dreams, it takes a fall.
Caught in stitches, knit and sprawl,
Threads entwine, a playful brawl.

In a cupboard, buttons hide,
Snickering at the thread's wild ride.
Sewing laughter, side by side,
Crafting chaos, no need to bide.

The Beauty of Fragile Connections

Strands of laughter weave through air,
Fingers dance without a care.
Snagged in stories, rich and rare,
Fragile bonds, a light affair.

Friendships bloom in silly ways,
Knotted ties that weave through days.
Spun from giggles, bright and gay,
They twirl and spin in sweet displays.

Layers of Memory Softly Weaved

Memories wrap like scarves in snow,
Each layer thick with joy's warm glow.
Tangles tickle, just so-so,
While laughter echoes 'round we go.

Once, a hat got caught up tight,
Floated like a kite in flight.
With every twist, a pure delight,
Fleeting moments shine so bright.

Serendipity Bound in Stitches

Threads tangled in playful dance,
A needle's jest, a thread's romance.
Laughter sewn in every seam,
A fabric patchwork of a dream.

Frogs in bow ties hop around,
In this cloth kingdom, joy is found.
Ticklish fabric pranks ensue,
Woven whimsy, oh so true!

Intricate Dreams Woven Softly

In a quilt where jesters play,
A sheepish grin leads the way.
Giggling threads that twist and twine,
Wrapped in giggles, truly fine.

Lions wear polka dot coats,
And every whimsy just promotes.
A tapestry full of smirks,
Where every fiber slyly lurks.

The Filigree of Enchantment

Dancing lace with winking eyes,
Crafting tales that start with pies.
A merry swirl of silly charms,
Hiding jokes in delicate arms.

Squirrels pirouette on the seam,
Playing tag in a fabric dream.
Unexpected twists, a feather's flight,
Tickles of laughter, pure delight.

Secrets Cloaked in Beauty

In shadows where mischief resides,
A spool of laughter always guides.
Secrets sewn beneath the light,
A playful cloak, oh what a sight!

Witty patterns play their part,
Whimsical stitches, a work of art.
Cloaked in charm and giggles galore,
Patchwork magic, forever more!

Whispers in the Weave

In a world of tangled threads,
Laughter hides in fabric beds.
A scarf whispers jokes so bold,
Woven stories, never old.

Lace curtains giggle in the breeze,
Tickling noses, making you sneeze.
A tangle of yarn runs from a cat,
Chasing shadows, oh, imagine that!

Fingers dance on a lacy quilt,
Spinning tales of laughter built.
Each stitch a chuckle, each knot a grin,
Sewing smiles where the fun begins.

When you peek through threads of dreams,
Laughter muffled, or so it seems.
Behind that fabric, joy is sewn,
In the weave, we find our own.

Lustrous Threads of Longing

Sparkling fibers that catch the eye,
Wink at you as they pass by.
Stitching wishes, thread by thread,
Sewing giggles in every bed.

A ribbon dances in delight,
Looping round, a little flight.
It whispers secrets to the lace,
Of mishaps and a silly face.

Oh, the patterns twist and twirl,
Creating mischief, making you whirl.
Lustrous strands of playful tease,
Who knew fabric could bring such ease!

In yarn's embrace, we find our cheer,
Telling stories for all to hear.
So pull that thread with giddy glee,
In this tapestry, we all agree.

Shadows of a Woven Heart

In the shadow of fibers spun,
Lurks a heart that loves the fun.
Braided laughter in every seam,
Woven wonders make us dream.

A patchwork quilt adorned with flair,
Bears the tales of love and care.
But watch out! The stitches tease,
As they play tag with your knees!

Lurking threads with naughty grins,
Entangled hobbies lead to spins.
Heart-shaped patterns in the art,
Whispers of joy that never part.

In the loom, our secrets hide,
A jester's cap, with joy inside.
So, dance with shadows in the heart,
In this web, we all take part.

Delicate Mask of Memory

A mask of lace that plays pretend,
Hiding giggles that won't end.
Memories sewn with a crafty hand,
Tickling thoughts that are so grand.

Each delicate fold tells a tale,
Of pranks and smiles that never fail.
Underneath, a memory stirs,
Of playful jokes and silly furs.

With threads that gleam like sunshine bright,
They dance and twirl, a lively sight.
Whispers of laughter, soft and clear,
In the fabric, joy is near.

So wear that mask and laugh aloud,
In the weave, we're all unbowed.
For memories wrapped in lace,
Bring back the fun in every place.

The Cloak of Hidden Truths

In shadows where secrets play,
A fabric grows wild each day,
Woven threads of giggles and grins,
Hide the chaos, let laughter spin.

A patchwork of all that we wear,
Stitched up with a dash of despair,
Oh, the stories this cloth could tell,
If only it didn't weave so well.

With ribbons that tease and delight,
It dances left, then sways right,
A costume of mirth, all askew,
What's the truth if I'm dressed like a zoo?

So come take a peek, lift a seam,
Find the oddities hiding, it seems,
Beneath the lace, a chuckle brews,
In disguise, we all play the fools.

Dreamscape of Whispering Fibers

In a dream where cotton clouds sing,
A tapestry of giggles takes wing,
Microphone mics made of tweed,
To spread the gossip, that's all we need.

Ribbons that rustle, they gossip aloud,
Enticing the mischief that's growing proud,
With threads of whimsy to stitch up a lie,
Who knew a scarf could keep secrets so spry?

Each knot is a tale of whimsical fun,
A quilt of quirkiness, oh what a run!
Tickling toes with a fuzzy "Boo!"
In this fabric world, what can't we do?

So let's dance in this wacky disguise,
Where the pillows have eyes and the blankets are wise,
Wrapped in the warmest silliness yet,
In this land of fiber, no rule is a threat.

Embracing the Delicate Hush

A whisper of lace feels shy,
Tickles the ears, oh me, oh my!
Wrapped like a taco, snug and tight,
In a quiet jest, we catch the light.

With frills galore and secrets to hide,
This charming cover is quite the ride,
A giggle escapes from the lace's embrace,
Who knew silence could have such a face?

Now watch as it flutters with grace,
In a game of peek-a-boo, we chase,
Feel that cheeky flick of the seam,
Where humor dances like in a dream.

Caught in the folds of this comedic delight,
Let hilarity be our guiding light,
In layers that hide, fun starts to unfold,
For laughter's the treasure, more precious than gold.

Cascades of Silken Wishes

Oh, the tales that silk can weave,
With dreams and giggles, who would believe?
Shimmering wishes float in the air,
Like kittens in costumes, beyond compare.

A cascade of laughter, draping the room,
In colorful threads that dance and bloom,
Purls in a row with a mischievous flair,
Concealing the funny, with style to spare.

Each fold holds a dream, each seam tells a pun,
A laughter explosion, we're just getting begun,
Through silken cascades, we secretly slide,
In this fabric of chuckles, our joy we confide.

So let's twirl in our garments of phobia-free fluff,
In this fabric fairyland, we can't get enough,
For in every stitch, there's a quirk to admire,
Wrap yourself up, let silliness inspire.

Flutters of a Timid Heart

A whisper caught in threads so fine,
A flutter starts, then sips the wine.
The lace around dances with a grin,
As hearts play hide and seek within.

A shy gaze darts, a laugh does flee,
Chasing dreams that tickle glee.
With every stitch, a secret shared,
This timid heart has unprepared!

Beneath this veil, a giggle lives,
With every twirl, the lace forgives.
A blush ignites, oh what a tease,
While fabric flourishes in the breeze!

The shyest smiles, a spark ignites,
In threads of joy, the heart delights.
Each flutter tells a tale so sweet,
In timid hearts, there's love to meet!

Secrets Bound in Stitches

A needle pricks where secrets dwell,
In every loop, there's a story to tell.
Tangled yarns in colors bright,
Hiding giggles in the moonlight.

Stitched up tight, but laughter breaks,
A giddy thread that never quakes.
Patterns drip with playful charms,
As secrets dance in restful arms.

Each knot a mishap, that's the fun,
Twirling tales when the day is done.
What lies beneath the fancy seams?
Just playful hearts and silly dreams.

With every seam, mischief thrives,
In this fabric, joy arrives.
What a mess, but oh so grand,
In stiched-up joy, we understand!

Tendrils of Hope in Ethereal Fabric

Floating strands in a dreamy weave,
Hidden giggles that dare to believe.
Whispers dance like playful sprites,
In tendrils of hope, mischief ignites.

Wavy paths that twist and curl,
Each loop a secret, a spin, a whirl.
Through the layers, a laugh ignites,
In the shimmers of starry nights.

Caught in a tangle, but who minds?
With winks and nudges, joy unwinds.
Ethereal fabric wraps a cheeky jest,
In features bright, we find our rest.

A tapestry of laughter and grace,
In every fold, we find our place.
When hope entwines with a wink so sly,
In this fabric, we'll dance and fly!

The Dance of Shadows and Lace

Beneath the beams where shadows play,
Laughter swirls in a lace bouquet.
With twinkling eyes, they come alive,
In the night where giggles thrive.

A pirouette, a somersault's cheer,
Hidden mischief, whispering near.
Rustling fabric in playful guise,
As laughter rings out under the skies.

Dancing figures with lacey bounds,
Tickling hearts, with shushy sounds.
Every twirl, a chuckle flows,
As shadows and lace tell jokes that rose.

So join the masquerade of delight,
Where stitches giggle through the night.
With every step, the dance's grace,
Shadows and lace, a playful chase!

Whispers of Delicate Threads

In a corner, a kitten plays,
Chasing shadows in silly ways.
With a toss, the lace takes flight,
A fluttering ghost in the light.

Grandma's lace on the carpet sprawls,
As the dog prances, then tumbles and falls.
"Oh dear," she mutters, knitting in hand,
"Can't keep my lace from becoming a band!"

Frogs in bow ties leap with glee,
Mistaking finery for a jubilee.
They croak sweet tunes, all awash with grace,
Dressed up for a fancy lace embrace.

Yet, the wind has its own plans, it's true,
Ruffling skirts and making quite a zoo.
Oh, the laughter that dances from lips,
As the lace gets caught in somersault flips.

Shadows Beneath Gossamer Dreams

Beneath a veil, the secrets grin,
As a squirrel tries to sneak in.
With tiny paws, it grabs a scrap,
Creating chaos—a furry mishap.

The moon peeks through, winks at the scene,
While a cat plots its heist, sly and keen.
It tangles in threads, stylishly bold,
Looking like royalty, or so we've been told.

Fairies giggle in the twilight air,
Dancing in lace without a care.
Their tiny shoes make sparkly sounds,
Lacing secrets in twirls around.

Oh, what a mess the moonlight makes,
With laughter shared, and the heart aches.
"More lace!" they cheer, in a whirl of delight,
Creating mischief till the morning light.

Enigma in a Tapestry

A tapestry hangs, so grand yet bizarre,
Holding tales of a very strange star.
With a twist here and a loop around there,
It conjures a cat doing the tango in air.

Knots of stories get tangled and spun,
As laughter erupts, who said it was fun?
A jester prances, tripping on thread,
Making everyone laugh till they're red.

In a garden of lace, the hedgehogs collide,
Rolling in thread, nowhere to hide.
They snicker and squeak, in playful attire,
"Who needs style when we play in the wire?"

What wonders arise from a simple design,
As friends come together, both feline and swine.
The stitches vibrate with giggles and cheer,
Unraveling stories we dare to endear.

Soft Echoes of Elegance

In a ballroom filled with shimmering lace,
A chicken struts with curious grace.
With a feathered top hat perched just right,
It twirls around, a comical sight.

The clock strikes twelve, and the floor explodes,
As the guests - a mix of furry and toads.
They glide and slide in a fanciful chase,
Creating a ruckus, oh what a space!

A rabbit appears, on a unicycle tight,
Spinning and wobbling, oh what a fright!
In its pockets, the secrets of gin,
Ready to toast to the fun that's within.

In the end, as the laughter wanes,
All that remains are the silly refrains.
With hearts aglow and spirits still high,
They dance through the evening, beneath the night sky.

The Elegance of Unraveled Dreams

Once a lady in a gown,
Slipped on a banana peel,
Spinning like a top she turned,
Leaving the crowd to squeal.

A dance of lace, it fell apart,
A whirlwind of fabric and flair,
With each twist, a bit of art,
She laughed, gave them all a scare.

Her shoes flew off, a grand ballet,
As onlookers gasped in delight,
The elegance of a comical fray,
Made her blush in the soft moonlight.

So next time you wear your best,
Beware the floors that may betray,
A potential slip in a lacey quest,
Could turn your ball into a play!

Threads of Shade and Light

In my closet hangs my frock,
A marvel for the eye to see,
But lo! A thread I cannot lock,
It dances whimsically like me.

I thought I'd dazzle at the ball,
But this dress has plans of its own,
With every step, it starts to sprawl,
Turning prance into a groan.

By candlelight, it twirls and spins,
Drawing laughter from all around,
A fabric full of mischief grins,
In threads of shade and giggles found.

Among the chatter, it made a friend,
A dapper tie that liked to sway,
Together they brought joy without end,
Threads of humor in bright array.

Textures of Forgotten Love

Once I stitched a heart so fine,
In velvet and with lace entangled,
But time unraveled every line,
With patterns that left us dangled.

A tale of kisses lost in seams,
Caught in the fabric of old regrets,
We danced to echoes of our dreams,
While the threads whispered sweet minuets.

Yet through the snags and awkward fluff,
Our memories turned to comic strips,
That lady's hat was quite the puff,
As we shared hearty, jovial quips.

So here we are, a patchwork puzzle,
With textures bold and laughs so loud,
Though love may fade in twisted tussle,
At least we wore the quirks proud!

Fragile Boundary of Perception

In a world of frills and frocks,
I dared to wear my grandma's dress,
But what was lace soon turned to shocks,
As I plummeted in excess.

A swing and a twist, oh what a sight,
The hem caught wind like a kite,
The fragile line of grace took flight,
While I wrestled with my inner plight.

The mirth of friends grew loud and bright,
As I transformed into a show,
In fabric's fancy, not a fright,
But a giggling mess, what a glow!

So if you venture out in style,
Just mind the edges of your dress,
For laughter can stretch a flexible mile,
And twirl you into lovely distress!

Whispers of Filigree Dreams

Under twinkling stars so bright,
A cat in a hat takes flight.
It trips on a thread of gold,
And giggles as the night unfolds.

A mouse with a monocle grins,
Joining in silly little spins.
They dance through a field of cream,
In a world that feels like a dream.

A quilted sky of patchwork fate,
Bunnies in bowties, oh, what a state!
Lace flies high like a kite in spring,
Together, they laugh at the joys they bring.

Shadows Danced in Silken Threads

A ghost in a gown made of lace,
Appears with a smile on its face.
It waltzes through shadows at night,
Tickling the stars with pure delight.

A spider spins tales, oh so frail,
While wearing its elegant veil.
It whispers sweet secrets to the moon,
As owls hoot a soft, silly tune.

The curtains sway with a giggly bounce,
As playful thoughts twist and flounce.
In this frolicsome dance, we find,
Laughter is the thread that binds.

Ethereal Embrace of Delicate Fabrics

A cherub wore socks of lace,
And flapped its wings in a jolly race.
It tripped on a little cloud,
And laughter swirled, oh so loud.

With ribbons that tangled in their tails,
They flew with the sounds of catchy gales.
A giggling breeze joined the fun,
As prancing threads began to run.

In fields of plush, they twirl and chase,
Tickled by the soft embrace.
In this quilt of dreams and cheer,
Funnies weave through atmosphere.

Lace-Laden Secrets of the Heart

A squirrel donned a lacey coat,
And swayed on a tree like a tiny boat.
It sang to the leaves with zest,
In a comedic woodland fest.

Tales of acorns and nutty tricks,
Were shared with a band of quirky flicks.
Rabbits chuckled with glee and delight,
As lace-clad creatures danced through the night.

The moon peeked behind fuzzy fur,
Enjoying the show with a soft purr.
In a whirl of laughter and art,
Lace threaded whims into the heart.

Reflections in a Gossamer Gaze

A mirror dressed in spider's thread,
Shows me a face that's better fed.
I dance with thoughts both light and grand,
With giggles escaping like grains of sand.

In moments shy, I toss disdain,
Like socks that vanish, causing pain.
Why does my hair think it can play?
Twirling wild in a funky ballet!

A wink from fate, a fleeting jest,
I pull the lace, it's like a test.
To trip on dreams or hold them tight,
As lace entangles with delight.

So here's to whims, to folly's pace,
To laughter hidden behind a face.
In gossamer winks and playful cheers,
We sway through giggles, scaring fears.

Whirls of Reverie in Silky Shadows

My thoughts do waltz in silky streams,
Like fabric tangling in my dreams.
With twirls and swirls, I skip the gloom,
Draped in distraction's vivid bloom.

I laugh at whispers of playful sighs,
That flutter like butterflies in disguise.
A secret dance with shadows near,
Each giggle a spark, igniting cheer.

The silliness of laced-up charms,
Wraps my senses in perfect arms.
They tease and taunt, a merry chase,
Leaving behind no time to erase.

A chorus of tricks in gentle tease,
Like lace that tickles, sure to please.
In whirls of reverie, I find my groove,
In every twirl, I can't help but move!

Breath of the Untold Stories

Behind the lace lies laughter's breath,
In tales of mischief, whispers of death.
Tell me a secret, just you and I,
Of how you adorned that pie in the sky!

The stories weave like threads of fate,
Each twist and turn, oh isn't it great!
With chuckles ripe from moments past,
And pantyhose that never last.

A fabric's dance, a fabric's wink,
I find my joy in every clink.
So let's regale of bobbles and lace,
In the breath of giggles, we'll find our place.

With stitches made of glee and wit,
These tales of ours are quite a hit.
So raise a glass and spin a yarn,
In this untold world, let laughter charm!

Cloaked in Threads of Intrigue

In whispers soft, the threads conspire,
To shroud my antics with playful fire.
Why do my shoelaces seek to roam?
They dance while I just want to go home!

Clothed in mystery, I strut with flair,
But my sweater's twisted, and it's not fair.
Each step I take brings giggles near,
As fabric fumbles and dreams appear.

The lace that binds my secret schemes,
Entangles loudly in silly beams.
Chasing echoes of tongue-in-cheek,
In threads of intrigue, the heart does peek.

So tiptoe lightly, oh sly old shoe,
Lest you reveal what you mustn't do.
In capes of humor and layers of grace,
We'll wrap this world in a laced embrace!

Dancers on Fabric Thrills

Beneath the fluttering folds, they prance,
With mischievous grins, they take their chance.
A twist, a twirl, a playful tease,
While fabrics swirl like autumn leaves.

Gossamer dreams in a fabric spree,
Tickling toes, oh, what glee!
Laughter wrapped in a silky embrace,
As dancers leap in a lacy race.

Snags and snickers, all in good fun,
A dance-off where everyone's won.
Tripping over threads, oh what a sight,
Leaving behind a giggle-filled night.

Chasing shadows on the textile floor,
With stitches that sing and seams that roar.
Lazy seams serve as slidey lanes,
When laughter rises and joy remains.

Revelation in Woven Relics

A tapestry whispers secrets of old,
With threads of humor, bright and bold.
Sneaky stitches and quirky designs,
Hide tales of time, like clownish signs.

Frayed edges peek with a cheeky grin,
Inviting all to join in the spin.
Warp and weft with a wink and a nod,
While laughter erupts like a playful plod.

In each woven corner, a joke to behold,
A pun on the fabric, quietly told.
Bound by stitches and stitched with flair,
Each thread a chuckle, floating in air.

Hiccups in lace lead to fits of glee,
A cloak of laughter, wild and free.
Revelations of giggles lagging behind,
In woven relics, joy intertwined.

Whispers of the Night's Caress

Moonlit shadows in silky flights,
Whispers of mischief among cozy nights.
Subtle sighs in fabric deep,
Where secrets gather, none dare to keep.

Night creeps softly with a chuckle near,
Tickling toes brings younger cheer.
A fuzzy blanket, a pajama dance,
Spinning tales of romance and chance.

Under borrowed beams, they hide and seek,
With goofy grins, they peek and speak.
Softly up-twirling in playful unrest,
While laughter glimmers, oh what a jest!

With lacey dreams stitched tight, they twine,
In moonlit threads, they twist and shine.
The night it tickles in humorous way,
Where whispers weave and giggles play.

Subtle Symphony of Intrigue

In the weave of laughter, a tune appears,
A symphony crafted of silken cheers.
Subtle notes of jests interlace,
Turning surprise into a cheeky chase.

Fabrics chatter in muted delight,
As playful threads dance through the night.
A glossy bow, a quirky trim,
When fabrics laugh, the chances brim.

Along the seams, secrets unfold,
Where mischief brews, oh so bold.
Fingers pluck at the strings of fate,
Creating jests we'll celebrate.

Lively plucks turn whispers to shrieks,
In this fabric world, humor speaks.
With every twist, a giggle ensues,
In this subtle symphony, we must choose.

Cosmic Threads in Fade

In stitches of the galaxy, we twirl,
With planets wearing socks, oh what a whirl!
Stars dance in tutus, spinning round and round,
While comets nibble cookies, oh my, how profound!

Floating through the cosmos, we chase lost dreams,
A nebula's giggle, bursting at the seams.
With humor stitched together, we can't be late,
As Saturn's rings laugh at their own fate.

Asteroids wear hats, quite the dapper sight,
While black holes sing ballads in the night.
Cosmic threads of laughter, woven with glee,
In this universe, chaotic, wild, and free.

Silken Hues of a Dusk Serenade

Draped in twilight's whimsy, shadows play chess,
With moonbeams giggling, nothing's a mess.
The night's a jester, wearing hues so bright,
As stars toss confetti in sheer delight.

Whispers of silk drift on the breeze,
While fireflies throw parties beneath the trees.
We dance with the colors, so wild and spry,
As the sun dips low, saying goodbye with a sigh.

Laughter's stitched with twilight's gentle glow,
Each laugh a petal, drifting soft and slow.
With silly serenades, we lose all our fears,
In the embrace of dusk, we toast with cheer.

Veil of Shadowed Fragrance

Beneath the cover, scents collide and spin,
Sneaky aromas claim a world within.
With garlic giggles and cinnamon's glee,
A fragrant dance floor where we all can be.

Lavender whispers secrets, oh so sly,
While roses poke fun as they flutter by.
In a canvas of laughter, perfumes run free,
As spice and sweet giggles mingle with glee.

Shadows chuckle softly, embracing the fun,
While scents weave tales 'til the morning sun.
In the garden of whimsy, we'll linger and roam,
Wrapped in laughter's tapestry, we find our home.

Entwined in Ethereal Silence

In a hush of giggles, the whispers unfold,
While secrets of silence weave stories untold.
A humor so subtle, yet brightly it glows,
In the realm of the quiet, the laughter just flows.

Caught in the stillness, shadows tease play,
While whispers of joy dance and sway.
Each pause a chuckle, a nod of delight,
In the comfort of quiet, we find our light.

Ethereal giggles wrap 'round like a mist,
In the silence we savor, can't bear to resist.
Entwined in the serene, we find the sweet jest,
As laughter and silence in harmony rest.

Gossamer Hues of Hidden Longing

A fluttering ghost in a fancy dress,
Sipping tea with a side of finesse.
Lace patterns dance like curious cats,
Spilling secrets that fall flat like hats.

When the wind sighs a cheeky tune,
The fabric giggles, a funny croon.
Tangled tales in pastel hues,
Tickling fancies like playful blues.

A clumsy flirt with lace in tow,
Trying hard not to steal the show.
And with a wink, they tell a joke,
As a startled dove takes flight and croaks.

In gossamer light, the pranks unfold,
With every swirl, a new tease told.
Sharing giggles in the afternoon,
While lace drapes dance, a charming boon.

Threads of Elegance and Enigma

In a world where lace knows no bounds,
A sock on a head is where humor's found.
Twisting threads in a giggly spree,
Spinning tales like a playful bee.

Dresses giggle when they're well-worn,
A silly dance in the early morn.
With each step, a delicate tease,
Threads whisper secrets riding the breeze.

Odd patterns make for silly sights,
As lacy visions claim the nights.
Jokes wrapped tightly in elegant seams,
Tickling fancies and wild daydreams.

In a tangled web, laughter ensues,
With twists and turns in colorful views.
While elegance giggles, bold and bright,
Threads of humor take glorious flight.

Enchanted Tapestry of Yearning

A tapestry woven with laughter and cheer,
Curtains that giggle when strangers are near.
Yarns that tickle dreams on the loom,
Dancing spirits fill empty rooms.

Hidden desires with a playful gleam,
A mischievous thread pulls on the seam.
When the hat falls off at last night's ball,
The whole world stops to have a good haul.

Puffs of lace float through the air,
Telling stories of love and dare.
Curled-up corners whisper and twirl,
While mischievous lace makes the heart swirl.

Every knot's a laugh shared in jest,
Woven together, we're oddly blessed.
As sparkles drift from each silly thread,
Yearning's a giggle, never quite dead.

Mystique of the Woven Whisper

Whispers of lace weave secrets around,
Tickling toes where laughter is found.
Under the chandeliers, giggles abound,
A dance of mischief in fabric renowned.

Each fold a mystery, lightly concealed,
Draped in fabric, adventures revealed.
With a silly wink that sets spirits free,
Threads rustle softly, like whispered glee.

In the cozy corners where lace likes to play,
Wink at the night, let the shadows sway.
A frolic of fun wrapped in a thread,
Secrets are shared, even perhaps bred.

So join the jest, don your finest lace,
Let surprises unfold at a light-hearted pace.
For in each twirl, find laughter's embrace,
As woven whispers bring smiles to place.

The Poetry of Hidden Layers

In a world so wrapped and tied,
A sock here, a bra there, where do I hide?
Each layer's a secret, a giggle or two,
Who knew my closet held a circus for you?

With slips and with frills, a mismatched array,
I find my naughtiness stowed far away.
A hundred of options, yet none can be seen,
Laughter erupts, oh, the joys of the unseen!

Tangled in lace, I'm a doll that's misfit,
In layers of chaos, it's hard to admit.
Every garment I own tells a tale of its own,
They whisper and giggle, but leave me alone!

With both ends of waistband just begging to meet,
I navigate fabric like dancing on feet.
A wardrobe so wild, it could pop at the seams,
Dressed up in layers, I'm lost in my dreams!

Twilight's Breath on Fabric

Beneath twilight's glow, with a grin on my face,
I twirl in the shadows, a fan of the lace.
A whisper of silk wrapped round in a swirl,
My antics exposed, like a mischievous girl.

Oh, the petticoats dance, they sway, and they sway,
Telling stories of parties gone wild yesterday.
With every twirl, I giggle, I laugh,
While the moon takes a peek at my lace-laden half.

In shadows I hide, yet the fabric reveals,
A world full of secrets, my heart it conceals.
As twilight insists, "Oh, come join the fun!"
I strike up a pose, letting laughter outrun!

The moon's silver glimmer, it tickles my toes,
In the drama of fabric, farce quickly grows.
What mischief we've made, with no end in sight,
Here's to veils of whimsy, in twilight's delight!

Corsetry of Emotion

Laced up tight in a corset of glee,
I'm squeezed into fun, like a marshmallow tree.
Every tug tells a story, each knot's a pun,
Who knew that my shape could bring all this fun?

As I cinch it down, I can't help but cheer,
For laughter and joy are the true corset here.
With every sigh, my heart starts to dance,
In this tight little bubble, I'm lost in a trance.

Ha! The irony stings, as I pinch and I pull,
Is it snugness or laughter that's making me full?
With every twist of fate, I'm decked in delight,
Corsetry unbound, let's party all night!

So here's to the fabric that hugs and disarms,
A waist full of chuckles and charming alarms.
In layers of joy that I choose to embrace,
I spin through this life, with a smile on my face!

Weavings of Unspoken Desires

In threads of the night, our secrets entwine,
Hidden thoughts flutter like moths to the shine.
With whispers of longing, they stitch and they tease,
In a fabric of giggles, they play with such ease.

What do you desire when lace is in view?
A tickle, a tease, or a notion or two?
The humor in longing can unravel the seams,
As we weave through our wishes, stitched close in our dreams.

The yarns of our hearts interlaced with glee,
Each twist and each turn sets our laughter free.
Oh, the fabric of jest wraps around every sigh,
In weavings of fun, we both soar and we fly!

So let's pull out the rolls, let's cut and create,
In the tapestry hung, let's weave and not wait.
For the fabric of whimsy, it stretches, it bends,
Together we'll laugh as the laughter transcends!

Arcana of Satin and Shadows

In a world of silk and thread,
Cats in costumes dance instead.
Laughter spills like spilled champagne,
As they prance through glittering rain.

A hat so tall it hits the sky,
With feathers floating way up high.
Pigeons in skirts are quite a sight,
Twisting their tails in pure delight.

Naptime's gone, no time for snooze,
Dancing now, we've nothing to lose.
Secrets whispered through the lace,
As the moon starts to join the race.

Bubbles float and laughter swells,
Daisies giggle, ringing bells.
In the shadows, stories play,
In this folly, who needs a bouquet?

Elysian Veils of Reverie

Within the folds where dreams reside,
Bunnies bounce, a silly ride.
With every hop and woeful wiggle,
The shadows giggle, and the daisies giggle.

A glasses swap brings quite the cheer,
As owls say, "Let's shift our gear!"
The air is thick with whimsy's grace,
As laughter exits every trace.

Cakes appear from nowhere fast,
As clowns dance, the die is cast.
Confetti storms of colored hue,
In foolish frolic, we find the crew.

When evening falls, the mischief grows,
As frocks become the starry clothes.
In this sense of pure delight,
We spin and twirl into the night!

Melodies of Fine Interlace

A tapestry of hints and winks,
Crooked hats and silly shrinks.
Socks with polka dots galore,
Clowns in slippers, what a score!

A lute that plays a merry tune,
While goats in jackets dance at noon.
In swirls of color, chaos reigns,
As joy bursts free, unbridled chains.

With every twist, the fabric squeaks,
While mice in bowties do their peaks.
Threads of laughter weave through air,
As everyone forgets despair.

Night reveals its playful side,
As mischief takes us for a ride.
In this merry tale we share,
The finest lace, without a care.

The Alluring Creep of Twilight

When shadows deepen, giggles grow,
As whimsical things scurry to and fro.
With capes that flutter in the breeze,
Monkeys swing from all the trees.

Sandal-wearing gnomes declare,
Who needs decorum, who needs flair?
With every laugh, a wild cheer,
As candlesticks begin to leer.

A fashion show of mismatched socks,
Lizards strut in diamond frocks.
As midnight chimes its funny rhyme,
Laughter echoes, freezing time.

As day bids night a playful farewell,
The moon joins in this goofy swell.
With smiles stitched beneath the stars,
It's fun and folly, just like ours!

The Gentle Touch of Mystery

A cloak of wonder drapes the night,
With giggles hidden just out of sight.
A peek reveals a dance so grand,
As mischief winks, with sleight of hand.

Frogs in top hats play charades,
While cats wear boots on midnight parades.
Each shadow holds a whispered sneer,
As laughter bubbles, then disappears.

A jester's hat upon the moon,
It beckons stars to join the tune.
A riddle wrapped in cotton candy,
With flavors bright and tastes so dandy.

So let the curious roam and prance,
In a world that spins and loves to dance.
For under every wink and glance,
A funny twist awaits romance.

Whirlwind in Tattered Petals

A storm of blooms spun round in cheer,
Petals fly like gossip in the air.
Butterflies play tag with the breeze,
While daisies chuckle with such ease.

A sunflower prances, tall and bright,
Waving hello to a bumblebee's flight.
The tulip twirls in a dress of spring,
As nature giggles, letting joy take wing.

Through gardens lush, where secrets bloom,
A gnome tiptoes, dodging the broom.
With shoes too big, he stumbles once,
And the daisies shake as he makes a punce.

So gather 'round the tattered laughs,
In every petal, a story brash.
Let the whirlwind sweep us away,
In floral jest, we'll forever play.

Stitched Secrets of the Heart

A needle pricks the fabric of dreams,
As seams unravel, bursting at the seams.
Hearts in pockets, stitched with care,
Each one hiding laughter, everywhere.

A button's missing, where could it be?
It rolled away to join a jamboree!
Threads of humor weave through the night,
As quips and jests take playful flight.

A patchwork soul, here and there,
With each new stitch, a quirky flair.
Secrets dance in every fold,
Woven tales that never grow old.

So let's sew stories with threads of glee,
In a quilt of giggles, just you and me.
For in each stitch, our laughter's the art,
With funny tales close to the heart.

The Quintessence of Transparency

In crystal halls where secrets gleam,
Ghosts of jesters plot and scheme.
A glass of joy, half full, half clear,
With bubbles bursting, visions appear.

Through windows wide, we gaze in awe,
At clumsy clowns without a flaw.
Their antics dance in the light of day,
As echoes of laughter lead our way.

With mirrors reflecting a world so bright,
Every giggle resounds like delight.
A juggler slips, and down he falls,
Glass shatters, but laughter befalls.

So raise your glass, toast to the fun,
To transparency, where pranks are spun.
In a realm where silliness reigns supreme,
We'll dance through life, living the dream.

Intricate Patterns of Love's Illusion

In shadows cast by frills and folds,
A jester dances, truth untold.
With every twirl, a secret prance,
Love giggles softly, takes a chance.

A string of pearls, a silly jest,
Whispers of hearts in fancy dress.
Amidst the lace, the tangle grows,
But who's the fool? Everyone knows!

Hearts wrapped up in silky strands,
Gaze upon the couple's plans.
Tickles at the edges, laughter bright,
Fools in love, what a sight!

Yet in this maze of soft delight,
No one can find the end in sight.
Fun in the chase, the chase is fun,
A game of hearts, all's said and done.

Veils of Mystery and Allure

At parties grand, behind a sheet,
A giddy heart feels quite the beat.
With every peek, a giggle shared,
What'd I see? Oh, I was spared!

The hidden clues, they twirl and spin,
As laughter swells, where to begin?
Whimsical hopes, the dance goes on,
A saucy wink, then they're all gone!

Beneath the fluff, absurdity reigns,
While lovers muse, they lose their brains.
A sly grin peeks, a lightening bolt,
Catch me if you can, this is no bolt!

With each sly glance, confusion grows,
Who is that? Oh, goodness knows!
In tangled webs, we spin and weave,
The laughter there, what shall we leave?

Celestial Threads in Moonlit Nights

The moon shines bright, a wink to all,
Love-fools wonder, will they stall?
With silk and dreams, a comical spin,
Twinkle toes where mischief begins.

A starry laugh, a bumpy ride,
Through layers soft, we'll seek and hide.
Fluffy giggles, the sky turns blue,
What's gravity, when love is true?

In this vast cosmos, hearts collide,
A beautifully tangled, absurd ride.
Yet tangled threads bring joy and cheer,
Through goofy paths, we persevere.

So let's embrace the cosmic jest,
We dance through moons, we jest the best.
With every stitch, our hearts take flight,
Night's laughter glows, it feels so right.

The Gentle Fall of Fragile Hopes

Like blossoms caught in gentle breeze,
Hopes tumble down with effortless ease.
Each flutter wraps a story told,
In lacey twists, the dreams unfold.

Chasing wishes, like butterflies,
In textured moments, laughter flies.
With every plummet from high above,
We catch the breaks, and speak of love.

Yet in this fall, oh what a sight,
A twist of fate, we laugh in spite.
With fragile dreams on a playful sway,
Laughter sings, come what may.

Through layers thin, we navigate,
With every giggle, we celebrate.
These silly hopes, they shall remain,
In tangled webs, our love's refrain.

Secrets Stitched in Gentle Patterns

In a corner of the room, quite a sight,
Lace curtains dancing in the moonlight.
A cat's caught in a web, what a show,
Chasing shadows, stealing the glow.

Grandma's secrets sewn into a quilt,
Each stitch a story, all neatly built.
But who knew the tea would spill so bold,
As laughter echoes, the tales unfold.

Hidden messages in every seam,
Of love gone wrong and a wild dream.
She claims she was once a daring spy,
But all she did was bake and sigh.

So when the lace begins to sway and twist,
Beware the secrets you didn't list.
For behind those threads of white and black,
Are tales of fun, and a playful hack.

Flickers of Light Beneath the Lace

A moth caught in the curtain's embrace,
Flashing bright in its fluttering race.
It thinks it's a night dancer, oh so proud,
But the lace laughs, covering all its shroud.

Sunlight filters through intricate holes,
Making shadows that play like trolls.
A game of hide-and-seek with the breeze,
While the chairs sit grumpy, refusing to tease.

Patterns made by light, a comic show,
Dancing decorations in a row.
Each shimmer tells tales of clumsy feet,
Turning the simple into a fun treat.

So let the light play its whimsical game,
With every flicker, it's never the same.
Underneath the lace, a laugh can chime,
Creating memories, one joke at a time.

Soft Echoes of Forgotten Wishes

Whispers of dreams tucked away tight,
Nestled in corners, out of sight.
Lace draping over wishes long past,
Like a pastry chef's secrets held fast.

What if wishes were made of cake?
Would they crumble or make us awake?
Laughter rings out as we chew and bite,
For every forkful holds a delight.

An old lady's sigh escapes the room,
About lost romances that ended in gloom.
But the lace giggles, it's seen it all,
From crushes that bloomed to utterly small.

So let's toast to hopes with a wink and a cheer,
For every wish that we hold dear.
Soft echoes laugh at our serious fuss,
In lace-covered dreams, it's always a plus.

Silhouette of a Starlit Design

At midnight, lace takes a playful bend,
Creating shapes of a mysterious friend.
A puppet show with stars in the mix,
As the moon laughs, lighting up tricks.

The night pulls patterns from dreams left behind,
Stitching together the tangled and blind.
A funny twist in every cosmic line,
Turns the ordinary into something divine.

As laughter colors the twilight sky,
Even the lace can't help but sigh.
Each fluttering edge holds a tale so bright,
Of shadowy dancers taking flight.

So join the party of whimsy tonight,
Beneath the designs that twinkle with light.
In the realm where laughter and lace intertwine,
Every silhouette sparkles, until we resign.

Veils of Yearning Serenity

In a world of fabric tumble,
Secrets hide with a giggle,
A wink beneath the draping cloth,
Where hearts can freely wiggle.

Lace frills dance with the breeze,
Tickling dreams of summer cheer,
But wait! What's this? A squirrel peeks,
With laughter, we pull it near.

Each thread a tale, oh so bright,
A rendezvous of fluttering souls,
Frolicking in mischief's light,
Barefoot on life's silly shoals.

A mask of lace, a playful guise,
Delusions wrapped in joyous folds,
As we stumble through our surprise,
Just wait till the story unfolds.

Echoes of Chiffon and Night

Beneath layers of fabric fluffy,
Whispers twirl and spark the air,
I find a cat with lady's hat,
And laugh away my midnight care.

Chiffon glimmers, moonlight glows,
Ballets of blunders swing and sway,
Yet in this charming, coat of prose,
A dance-off in pajamas play!

Heels are high but grace is low,
A twisted ankle brings a cheer,
The night alive with chaos flow,
The laughter loud, ridiculous, clear.

The fabric plays a merry tune,
As mishaps weave a comical scene,
With each step, we share a swoon,
In dreams of silk, a night unseen.

Layers of Silk and Solitude

In the starlit night, I slip,
Through layers of a silky cloak,
A ghostly waltz, an awkward trip,
I laugh, as if it's just a joke.

Beneath the whispers, silky swells,
Lurks a snicker, waits to break,
A jest of lace that softly yells,
As I dance with my own mistake.

Menacing shadows wiggle, play,
My solitude, a jester's hat,
With giggles muffled, I sway and sway,
Who knew silence could go splat?

Laughter echoes in my heart,
As mischief sails on gossamer seas,
In every layer, a funny part,
Who knew solitude could tease?

The Art of Enigmatic Embrace

Lace speaks softly, secrets swirl,
Like misplaced socks on laundry day,
With giggles, in confusion's twirl,
We trip along this lacy way.

An embrace of fabric, weirdly stitched,
In tangled hugs, we find our place,
With humorous twists, our minds quite switched,
Who knew hugs could hide such grace?

We dance a dance no one has learned,
In laughter, fabric comes alive,
Around each corner, joy returns,
With every twirl, we laugh and strive.

The art of jest, a crazy play,
In lopsided leaps, we find our fun,
In every fold, we make our way,
Unearthing joy as the day is done.

Folds of Forgotten Whispers

In the closet where secrets hide,
A sock and a glove play side by side.
They giggle and laugh, causing such a fuss,
Dreaming of days when they danced on the bus.

The dust bunnies chat, their tales unconfined,
Plotting adventures, oh what a bind!
They whisper of crumbs, both tasty and sweet,
But always get caught by vacuum's quick feet.

Old hats on a shelf, with stories to sell,
One claims he was once a captain so swell.
But tripping on feathers, he fell with a thud,
Oh, what a mess from the hat's little bud!

And so, with each fold, tales tumble and spin,
In the wardrobe of laughter, where giggles begin.
Each whisper forgotten, yet fleeting in time,
The hilarity grows, like a comical rhyme.

Crescendo of Lace Kisses

A ladybug's blush on a lace-covered shoe,
Stealing soft glances and scooting on through.
She dances on petals, a boogie so spry,
While bees hum a tune, oh my, oh my!

The ruffles on skirts twist and swirl in the breeze,
Tickling the ankles of gigglers at ease.
A misstep, a tumble, a cupcake in hand,
Laughter erupts, it's a sugary stand!

As lace prances lightly, mischief takes flight,
A parade of oddities gracing the night.
With every lace kiss, a chuckle ignites,
In a tapestry woven of whimsical sights.

Thus the evening unfolds in a waltz of delight,
With clinks of the glasses, and friends, oh so bright.
Each lace stitch a pause in the jovial glee,
A crescendo of laughter, come join the spree!

The Embrace of Gentle Fragments

A button once lost, now found in the fray,
Huggles a needle, who's gloomy today.
Together they sip on thread's tangled brew,
Sharing soft stories of fabric they knew.

Frayed edges of sanity flutter and tease,
While patches of color whisper to please.
Each snip of the scissors, a giggle resounds,
In the quilt of life's mishaps, joy knows no bounds.

The ribbons all tangle, but don't mind the fuss,
Singing sweet songs of a glorious plus.
With ties that won't sever, they twirl in the air,
Creating a ruckus that sparks unaware.

In a box full of fragments, the mishaps collide,
But laughter embraces, they chuckle with pride.
For every loose end, a tale shall ignite,
In the dance of misfits, life's truly polite!

Interwoven Tales of Innocence

A kitten in lace, what a curious sight,
Pouncing and prancing, her landing's a fright.
With mischief in paws and crumbs in her fur,
A whirlwind of joy, oh, how she will stir!

The daisies all giggle as she bumbles about,
While the clouds in the sky give a jovial shout.
They rain down confetti on soft velvet grass,
As laughter erupts from the ones who just pass.

A pirate's lost eye patch turns into a hat,
Worn by a dog, who thinks he's quite that!
He struts down the lane like a captain with pride,
But trips over pebbles, oh what a wild ride!

Each moment a treasure, every glance a delight,
Interwoven tales in the warm autumn light.
With innocence wrapped in the fabric of play,
Life's funny adventures dance all through the day!

Secrets in Stitched Shadows

Whispers of fabric, secrets unfold,
Fingers in stitches, tales to be told.
A cat in the corner, just plotting away,
While lace ruffles giggle, come join in the play.

Lurking in corners, a mouse does a dance,
Spinning in circles, in a lacy trance.
Winks from the curtain, they think I can't see,
As breadcrumbs scatter, wild and carefree.

Birds tease the branches with beaks made of thread,
And humor takes flight where the fabric is spread.
With each woven whimsy, a smile's set to bloom,
In shadows of stitches, joy fills the room.

Life's little quirks in a lacy embrace,
They giggle and whisper, light-hearted with grace.
So let's grab some needles, and join in the fun,
In this fabric world, we're never outdone.

Muse of Frayed Edges

A thread unwinds, what mischief it plans,
With frayed little edges, it spritzes like fans.
Laughter erupts from a tangled spool,
As fabric and chaos conspire at the school.

A hem that is loose wears a floppy old grin,
While buttons leap forth, ready to spin.
Socks play hide-and-seek, under beds they do scoot,
As threads thread the needle, what a silly hoot!

Dancing around with a lighthearted cheer,
Those fraying seams whisper, "Hey, we're still here!"
Patchwork of giggles, they bring such delight,
In seams made for laughter, we dance through the night.

Buttons pop off to share tales of their fate,
In the drawer of wonders where we celebrate.
So let's embrace quirks, the mix-up, the jest,
For behind those frayed edges, we're truly the best.

The Lacework of Illusions

Look here, a lace curtain, is it just a guise?
As gnomes in the garden, they plot and they rise.
Spinning yarns tighter than a well-kept dear,
In threads of bright colors, the laughter draws near.

Ladders of fancy, they sway and they bend,
As lace magically dances, it's laughter we send.
A spider's bizarre move, a tango so grand,
In the knots that are formed, conjure up a band!

The secrets they hide are playful but sly,
With winged insects buzzing, they share a sweet pie.
As fluffles of fabric wave in the breeze,
They tell all the stories that tickle and tease.

So hold onto your haunches, the fun's just begun,
In lacey disguises, we laugh and we run.
With each swirl and twirl, let the giggles chime on,
In this lacework of life, we'll continue till dawn.

Veils of Ephemeral Grace

Twist and tangle, oh what a sight,
Veils dancing lightly, in the moon's silver light.
Frolicking shadows, they leap and they sway,
With laughter cascading, they steal hearts away.

A wink from the curtain, a giggle ensues,
While ribbons are ruffled, sharing their views.
Poking out fingers, they tickle the air,
As the dance of the veils spreads joy everywhere.

Each twist tells a story, each frill holds a cheer,
As giggly reflections bounce here and then there.
In the glow of the night, where the whimsy takes flight,
Lively veils whisper, "Oh come join the night!"

So sway to the rhythm, let laughter resound,
With veils made of whimsy, where joy can be found.
In the ephemeral grace of this playful charade,
We'll frolic together, in the bliss we create.

www.ingramcontent.com/pod-product-compliance
Lightning Source LLC
Chambersburg PA
CBHW060123230426
43661CB00003B/316